150 Uplifting Quotes from Remarkable Cancer Survivors

Phil Collins

Copyright © 2023 Phil Collins

All rights reserved. No part of this publication may be reproduced, distributed, or transmitted in any form or by any means, including photocopying, recording, or other electronic or mechanical methods, without the prior written permission of the publisher, except in the case of brief quotations embodied in critical reviews and certain other noncommercial uses permitted by copyright law.

Dedication

Dedicated to all those who bravely faced the battle against cancer, may these inspiring words from remarkable survivors offer strength, hope, and courage on your journey.

Table of Contents

Introduction

In this collection, it present 150 powerful and uplifting quotes from incredible individuals who have conquered the formidable challenge of cancer.

Their resilience, wisdom, and unwavering spirit shine through these pages, offering a beacon of hope and encouragement to anyone facing this arduous journey.

Each quote serves as a testament to the strength of the human spirit and the unwavering determination to overcome adversity.

It is my sincere wish that these inspiring words provide comfort, motivation, and solace to those navigating their own path through the trials of cancer.

Cancer quotes from Super Survivors

1. "Being a cancer survivor is like being shaken in a kaleidoscope. You grasp for your bearings, desperate to find your balance amidst the chaos. When the dust finally settles, there is a new constellation of colors that are magical and beautiful."
- Renee Exelbert

2. "Remember that all cancers are not the same. Take each day as it comes and spend time doing things you enjoy with your loved ones."
- Robin Squellati

3. "It's a choice to see joy. Choose it. It's really easy to let the severity and awfulness of your diagnosis take over, but you can choose to acknowledge things are bad, but then focus your energy on even the tiniest blessings until you see more and more each day you're able to be here, whether that's 50 days or 50 years."
- Kristina Kotlus

4. "Overcoming cancer awakens a courage and confidence inside of you that makes you want to live big, bold and intentional every day. It becomes much easier to grow as a person, because you have already been forced way out of your comfort zone. I don't worry about failing when I try new things now, because my inner voice always reminds me that 'this' can't be any harder than cancer!"
– Renee Ward

5. "I learned how to look at each silver lining without feeling like I was falling for a Hallmark card. 'Everything happens for a reason' was still hard to hear, but it became the only way I could survive when the bad news kept coming. Ultimately, I realized what a miracle it really is to be alive and to lean into mindfulness, being present, as the best remedy for truly enjoying life."
- Stephanie Chuang

6."When you are diagnosed, surround yourself with the best medical providers and uplifting friends. Going through cancer is scary and you can easily go down a path of negativity and darkness. But you can't let yourself do that. You need to have positivity and encouragement from others. It truly does help you through your healing."
- Charlotte Shaff

7."Once you see the world through the cancer lens, you realize how many people are going through challenges and that you are never truly alone."
- Cynthia Hayes, cancer survivor, patient advocate and author of The Big Ordeal: Understanding and Managing the Psychological Turmoil of Cancer

8."I believe in life, no matter the circumstances, no matter what you are facing. You only have two choices. You can lay down and die, or you can get up and live! I choose life! I don't want to be in this club and neither does my mother, father, sister or brother, but we all thank God we are. We are survivors."
- Barry Davis

9. "I am grateful to be alive and still have the quality of life which makes it possible for me to spread awareness related to the benefits of detecting prostate cancer early."
- Mical J. Roy

10. "Cancer recovery is hard work. Life is hard work. And it really pays off. Hang in there."
- Helen Szablya

11. "Cancer is different for every person it affects. My advice? Get the latest information. Talk to doctors. Talk to friends and others who have had what you have. Read articles and educate yourself so you can be an active participant in your treatment."
- Ian Mair

12. " I feel so grateful for the family and friends that surrounded me during that difficult time. It pains me that there are so many men who don't have the same resources or support system as I did."
- Jeffrey Wilde

13. "Beating cancer has been a team effort for me. I couldn't have done it, and I can't continue to fight it, without help. But it all starts with me, a cancer survivor. It all starts with me trying to help others become cancer survivors too."
- Al Wallace

14."Cancer is deadly serious. I urge you to do whatever it takes to survive. Make your choices based on what you believe is best for you, your body, and your future. In this way, any treatment you choose will have the best possible effectiveness it can produce."
– Heidi Bright, author of Thriver Soup: A Feast for Living Consciously During the Cancer Journey

15. "Before cancer I had this feeling that I was owed a certain level of happiness. After surviving cancer I realize we're owed nothing, not even time, so I try to live in a state of appreciation. It's difficult, but I have to tell you when you're looking outside the window of a hospital room all the things we get tangled up in mean very little. So, be present and choose to be grateful."
- JP Faiella

16. "It took me seven years to realize I wasn't alone. I believed for seven years that I was the only 20-something with cancer in New York City."
- Matthew Zachary, Stupid Cancer Founder

17. "Getting diagnosed with breast cancer at a young age, unveiled the meaning of life by removing the safety blanket I was wrapped in. I understood very quickly that life has a time limit, and because of this now ticking clock, I am able to live my life fully every single day, filling it only with things that bring me joy. We have one shot at this lifetime, live it fully."
- **Dana Donofree**, CEO + Founder of AnaOno

18. "Cancer does not define who I am, although it is a significant part of me and who I am becoming."
– **Carrie Kreiswirth**

19."I remember being in the treatment room and looking around and seeing all the sick people. I then got home and looked in the mirror and realized I was also one of those sick people. A few days later my sister Leah brought over this beautiful lipstick, I put it on and looked at myself and saw the real me. That person I once knew, and knew would get through this,"
- Sarah Kelly, Co-Owner of SaltyGirl Beauty.

20."I always say, the darkest period of your life may actually reveal a beautiful gift. Be it family, friends, a new way you want to live your life or even letting go of toxic people/ things in your life. Stay open during illness to look for these gifts. They are there."
- Cynthia Besteman, Owner and Founder of Violets Are Blue.

21. "When I was diagnosed with a mild form of lymphoma, I thought to myself, OK, this is going to be a new chapter in my life. And I decided to take that literally by doing a lot of writing while I was going through my chemotherapy sessions. During the chemo sessions, I finished two spy stories that I has started writing many years before the diagnosis, and I also wrote the text of a book designed to become a children's picture book about a new kind of SuperHero who could help make the world a much safer place for us all."
– Robert Barrows

22. "Every day is a gift. You have to find those things to be grateful for."
– Susan Webster

23. "I relied on my faith in God and the power of prayer to pull me out of some of my darkest moments. I recently thanked my Mom again for introducing me to Christ as He was my rock. Since those times, I've lived with so much more fervor, an immense gratitude and peace that I can't describe."
- **Cashmere Nicole**, Founder of Beauty Bakerie

24. "Attitude is everything when you're trying to heal."
– **Stephanie Jackson**

25. "There's no greater weapon in your personal fight against cancer than focusing on your joy. I made a decision early on — that I could either have cancer and be miserable, or have cancer and be full of joy whenever physically possibly. Loving life and being present in every moment you're lucky enough to share with family and friends will not only help you defeat cancer, but will keep you focused on what matters while you're beating it."
– Julie Stokes

26. "Your loved ones want to give you what you need right now. Tell them!"
– Noel Van Dyke

27. "I had just graduated from grad school at age 24 when I was diagnosed with cancer. In an instant the life I had planned for myself fell away. During my chemo treatments, my girlfriend and I read books and watched movies about potential cancer causes. We learned about risk reduction, and diet. She created a simple website and social media accounts sharing what we had learned. In the years since we have helped 1.5 million people learn more about health. We created a global brand, and have met with so many survivors. The life I had planned fell away, but the life I was meant to live became clear. It sounds cliche to say 'your worst day can be your best day' - but I am living proof."
-Michael Kuech, Co-Founder of Your Super

28. "Today I will surrender to things I can't control."
– Patricia Heitz

29. "There's no need to wait for the bad things and b.s. to be over. Change now. Love now. Live now. Don't wait for people to give you permission to live, because they won't."
– Kris Carr

30. "Facing cancer forces you to look inward, ask yourself hard questions about life, death, purpose, and gratitude, and it enables a new depth and understanding of how to live life from your heart, following your soul's purpose."
– Sally Morgan

31. "A cancer diagnosis can be thought of as a turning point to set you free to fulfill or examine your dreams and passions. It is a time to feel infinite strength while being prompted to look inside yourself not only for ways to cope but for secrets to your own happiness."
– Diana Raab

32. "If you can stay strong for your family, you can stay strong for yourself."
– Dan Barba

33. "Keep your faith to God, to your family, and to yourself. There is no other better way to fight cancer when you know that there are lives around you that fight beside you. They help and give you reason to move, translating to your positive view about life."
– Aaron Simmons

34. "Appreciate the little things. Feel the flowers, the sky, the breeze, the love of your family. This helped me to enjoy that chapter of my life and face my disease as a door that opened my eyes to a new view of the world."
- Daniel Carter

35. "I'm stronger than I thought I was. My favorite phrase has been, 'this too shall pass.' I now understand it really well."
– **Robin Roberts**

36. "Our life doesn't end the minute we get that diagnosis. We still have some living to do."
- **Shannon Doherty**

37. "I think after overcoming breast cancer, you sort of become fearless and somehow going up to your boss to talk about a possible promotion doesn't seem like such a daunting task anymore."
-Hoda Kotb

38. "My scars? I barely see them. I feel whole; I really do. Because every day, I get to say, 'There's no cancer.' I'm healthy, and that's beautiful."
- Wanda Sykes

39. "'Everything will be OK in the end. If it's not OK, it's not the end.' Ever since I was diagnosed with breast cancer, this quote has been my mantra. These words have been my anthem, my inspiration, my comfort and my prayer."
- Giuliana Rancic

40. "I laughed more in the hospital than I ever have in my life, making fun of all the weird things that were happening to me. My friends would walk in with this sad look, and I would throw something at them and say, 'Come on! This isn't the end of the world!'"
- Christina Applegate

41. "Try to find the moments in your day
that give you joy and give you happiness,
because there's still time to laugh, and
life is going on."
- Rita Wilson

42. "It takes hard work, it takes
determination, you have to be relentless,
you have to work through the tears and
the pain and all that kind of stuff. But
you can't do any of that without the
people who love you and support you."
- Kylie Minogue

43. "I don't have breasts—so why do I have to pretend like I do? That stuff isn't important. I'm just grateful to have been born at a time when the research made it possible for me to survive. I feel so incredibly lucky to be alive."
- **Kathy Bates**

44. "My lesson was, in my diagnosis and laying on the radiation table every single morning for seven weeks, that nobody can take care of me but me. And I wasn't doing that ... I had to reflect and had to remember who it was I came in as and had to really sort of redefine my life."
- **Sheryl Crow**

45. "I'm not someone who likes looking back. I look forward to it. That's how I operate. We'll finish an episode, and I am just ready for the next thing. I'm always just moving on, you know?"
- Julia Louis-Dreyfus

46. "I am positive about my life and about my journey, and I hope that I can touch other people to be positive about theirs ... I'm happy if I'm entertaining people, but I'm happiest when I'm helping people."
- Olivia Newton-John

47. "Life's better now. Maybe it was meant to happen for many reasons, because my life in many ways is richer."
- Giuliana Rancic

48. "I remember thinking, 'I will do anything and everything I need to do to stay alive for my daughter and make sure this has the least amount of impact on her life.' ... There are a lot of young moms going through this and I want them to know, 'Hey, I can do this too!'"
- Jessica St. Clair

49. "My life passed over me like a big wave, and after, I was left there standing. This turned out to be a very good thing. I stopped. I looked at my life, I looked at my body and spirit. I got a new perspective. That's brought me incredible clarity and a lot of peace."
- Melissa Ethridge

50. "Obviously, it wasn't meant for me to die of cancer at 40. Every day my life surprises me, just like my cancer diagnosis surprised me. But you roll with it. That's our job as humans."
- Edie Falco

51. "Don't sit around playing Mr. Tough Guy. Don't say 'It's going to go away.' It's just important, just go get checked out. It's not like you're going to lose your manhood."
- Peter Criss

52. "I've always thought of myself as being a warrior. When you actually have a battle, it's better than when you don't know who to fight."
- Carly Simon

53. "It's very important to keep your mind busy with positive events and activities and the like. The most important truth? You start looking at every day in a more profound way."
- Diahann Carroll

54. "The only thing we have to fear is fear itself. So the only thing to really be afraid of is if you don't go get your mammograms."
- Cynthia Nixon

55. "I think a lot of the times when you get to a high level of competition, it becomes the most important thing in the world and it's really not. There is a big life outside of sports."
- Eric Shanteau

56. "The cancer served a real purpose, making me a little bit more conscious of time."
- Gloria Steinem

57. "Cancer no longer rules my life — I'm getting back to myself. I'm healed as much as anybody who's gone through this can be, and I will continue to support and fight alongside my sisters. Once you're in this family, you're in for life."
- Sandra Lee

58. "The decision to have a mastectomy was not easy. But it is one I am very happy that I made. My chances of developing breast cancer have dropped from 87 percent to under 5 percent. I can tell my children that they don't need to fear they will lose me to breast cancer ... On a personal note, I do not feel any less of a woman. I feel empowered that I made a strong choice that in no way diminishes my femininity."
- Angelina Jolie

59. "When you hear those three words, 'You have cancer' — wow — that's coming face to face with your mortality. You never think that you're not here forever."
- Suzanne Somers

60. "A huge part of my success as an athlete was that I had the mental game. To get through the toughest moments of treatment I relied on goal setting and keeping that positive mentality."
- Shannon Miller

61. "As I've told my friends who've also been treated for breast cancer, I've joined The Club — not one I wanted to join or even thought I would ever be joining — but here I am ... Medical diagnoses can leave you feeling alone and scared. When it comes to breast cancer you're not alone, and scary though it is, there's a network of amazing women to help you through it."
- **Judy Blume**

62. "It was a newfound level of support when I started to speak with other survivors ... Knowing that they got to the other side, I knew that I too could get there."
- **Samantha Harris**

63. "A couple years ago I got breast cancer, and that was a good test, because I always said I'm not afraid of dying. And I wasn't. I mean, I felt, God, I've just joined a family of millions of women who have gone through this. And how interesting. What a journey this is going to be."
- Jane Fonda

64. "It's a life-changing thing to be in a position of needing help and being so lucky as to get it. And to feel like that's okay. You can't just take care of everybody else all the time. That's almost as perspective-changing as the illness. For someone like me, that was kind of tough."
- Maura Tierney

65. "I am a better parent. I yell less and cuddle more with my daughters. I am a better wife. I yell less and choose my words more carefully, remembering we are what we say. I want to leave every room I enter better than the way I found it. I'm not saying cancer is a gift — because if it was I would gladly return it — but now that the box has been opened, so have my eyes and my heart."
- **Amy Robach**

66. "The only thing certain was the uncertainty. All I could do was realize my strength and play my game better. This realization made me submit, surrender and trust, irrespective of the outcome, irrespective of where this takes me, eight months from now, or four months from now, or two years."
- **Irrfan Khan**

67. "I probably ended up where I needed to be. Those are the things, when you fight a life-changing battle, that you contemplate — and maybe you would never have contemplated them otherwise. So, when you contemplate those things it sure does focus you on what you want to do with the rest of your life."
- Joan Lunden

68. "Cancer didn't bring me to my knees, it brought me to my feet."
- Michael Douglas

69. "One of my doctors suggested I start going to a facility that wasn't the closest to me, but closest to the ocean. I arranged to meet a pal every day after my treatment and that would make us feel wonderful. There's nothing more gratifying than the ocean for me. It's very important to keep your mind busy with positive events and activities and the like. The most important truth? You start looking at every day in a more profound way."
- Diahann Carroll

70. I didn't think it was anything serious because years ago I felt a lump and it was benign. I assumed this would be too. It kind of takes the wind out of your sails, 'My energy is coming back. S*it happens. I ought to pull myself together a bit."
- Maggie Smith

71. "Don't be scared. Be positive. Take the right advice and act as soon as you can. If there's an issue in your system, don't ignore it."
-Yuvraj Singh

72. "We have all been thrown down so low that nobody thought we'd ever get up again; but we have been long enough trodden now; we will come up again, and now I am here."
- Sojourner Truth

73. "Life is to be lived, not controlled;
and humanity is won by continuing to
play in face of certain defeat."
- Ralph Ellison

74. "The triumph can't be had without
the struggle."
- Wilma Rudolph

75. "We must embrace pain and burn it
as fuel for our journey."
- Kenji Miyazawa

76. "Since I had cancer I've realized that
every day is a bonus."
- Geoffrey Boycott

77. "Yesterday I dared to struggle. Today
I dare to win."
- Bernadette Devlin

78. "Cancer opens many doors. One of
the most important is your heart."
- Greg Anderson

79. "I think cancer is a hard battle to fight alone or with another person at your side, but I will say having someone to pick you up when you fall, stand by your side through every appointment and delivery of bad news, is priceless."
- Jenna Morasca

80. "The most important thing in illness is never to lose heart."
- Nikolai Lenin

81. "I'm in good shape. My cancer means
I have lost a lot of organs and I'm a lot
lighter. I have devoted myself to yoga and
I'm doing handstands."
- Eve Ensler

82. "Working out is my way of saying no
to cancer, 'You're trying to invade my
body; you're trying to take me away from
my daughters, but I'm stronger than you.
And I'm going to hit harder than you."
- Stuart Scott

83. "You know, once you've stood up to cancer, everything else feels like a pretty easy fight."
- David H. Koch

84. "You can be a victim of cancer, or a survivor of cancer. It's a mindset."
- Dave Pelzer

85. "I'm battling cancer. It's another battle I intend to win."
- Arlen Specter

86. "Cancer is a word, not a sentence."
- John Diamon

87. "I want to see cancer cured in my
lifetime. It might be."
- James D. Watson

88. "Strength is born in the deep silence
of long-suffering hearts; not amidst joy."
- Felicia Hemans

89. "We have two options, medically and emotionally: give up or fight like hell."
- Lance Armstrong

90. "Now I'm fighting cancer, everybody knows that. People ask me all the time about how you go through your life and how's your day, and nothing is changed for me."
- Jim Valvano

91. "Once cancer happens it changes the
way you live for the rest of your life."
- Hayley Mills

92. "When someone has cancer, the
whole family and everyone who loves
them does, too."
- Terri Clark

93. "Time is shortening. But every day that I challenge this cancer and survive is a victory for me."
- Ingrid Bergman

94. "I want men to know that things really do get better — and they get better fairly rapidly. Don't get discouraged."
- George Campbell

95. "Attitude is a little thing that makes a
big difference."
- Winston Churchill

96. "Some days there won't be a song in
your heart. Sing anyway."
– Emory Austin

97. "Oh, my friend, it's not what they take away from you that counts – it's what you do with what you have left."
– Hubert Humphrey

98. "There is no hope unmingled with fear, no fear unmingled with hope."
– Baruch Spinoza

99. "Optimism is the foundation of
courage."
– Nicholas Murray Butler

100. "The human spirit is stronger than
anything that can happen to it."
– C.C. Scott

101. "Courage is not the absence of fear,
but rather the judgment that something
else is more important than fear."
– Ambrose Redmoon

102. "Cancer can take away all of my
physical abilities. It cannot touch my
mind, it cannot touch my heart, and it
cannot touch my soul."
– Jim Valvano

103. "You never know how strong you are until being strong is the only choice you have."
- Cayla Millis

104. "Cancer is that awful word we all fear when we go to the doctor for a physical exam, but in that brief dark moment we hear it the world we live in and the people we share it with begin to illuminate things we did not even pay attention to."
– BD Phillips

105. "I have heard there are troubles of more than one kind. Some come from ahead and some come from behind. But I've bought a big bat. I'm all ready you see. Now my troubles are going to have troubles with me."
- Dr. Seuss

106. "Toughness is in the soul and spirit, not in muscles."
- Alex Karras

107. "Life is without meaning. You bring the meaning to it. The meaning of life is whatever you ascribe it to be. Being alive is the meaning."
— Joseph Campbell

108. "Now I've thought of another: Never give up. Never surrender."
- Jason Nesmit

109. "The only disability in life is a bad attitude."
- Scott Hamilton

110. "In terms of fitness and battling through cancer, exercise helps you stay strong physically and mentally."
- Grete Waitz

111. "The important thing is not how many years in your life but how much life in your years."
- Edward J. Steilglitz

112. "Enjoy the little things, for one day you may look back and realize they were the big things."
- Robert Brault

113. "Cancer is not a straight line. It's up and down."
- Elizabeth Edwards

114. "A positive attitude may not solve all your problems, but it will annoy enough people to make it worth the effort."
- Herm Albright

115."Cancer is messy and scary. You throw everything at it, but don't forget to throw love at it. It turns out that might be the best weapon of all."
- Regina Brett

116. "To fear is one thing. To let fear grab you by the tail and swing you around is another."
- Katherine Paterson

117. "When you come to the end of your rope, tie a knot and hang on."
- Franklin D. Roosevelt

118. "During chemo, you're more tired than you've ever been. It's like a cloud passing over the sun, and suddenly you're out. You don't know how you'll answer the door when your groceries are delivered. But you also find that you're stronger than you've ever been. You're clear. Your mortality is at optimal distance, not up so close that it obscures everything else, but close enough to give you depth perception. Previously, it has taken you weeks, months, or years to discover the meaning of an experience. Now it's instantaneous."
- Melissa Bank

119. "There can be life after breast cancer. The prerequisite is early detection."
- Ann Jillian

120. "One of the things that can help people with cancer is having something that you really look forward to doing, so that you can focus on that while the treatments are going on. I guess it's like saying, 'I have unfinished business left before I die."
- Joe Marelle

121. "Nah. I'm a tough cookie. Except for
the cancer, I'm fine."
- Lisa Scottoline

122. "Only in the darkness can you see
the stars."
- Martin Luther King Jr.

123."Cancer gave me an understanding of the point of all this. To survive. Most of our lives it is easy but for the moments when it becomes difficult, when accident or sickness or sadness strikes, it's just about remembering one thing. You must simply survive."
- Shaun Hick

124. "I do not wish my anger and pain and fear about cancer to fossilize into yet another silence, nor to rob me of whatever strength can lie at the core of this experience, openly acknowledged and examined... imposed silence about any area of our lives is a tool for separation and powerlessness."
- Audre Lorde

125. "I felt great empathy for my friend, as one form of cancer after another emerged to challenge him. I felt sympathy for his suffering that surely clawed at his daily routines, always active and busy, but he rarely verbalized complaints while courageously challenging his archenemy. He met pain and physical decline with 600-calorie workouts; he discarded anxieties somewhere along innumerable running trails; he faced death by running through life at full stride."
- Brent Green

126. "Who can say they have been through cancer twice and beat it? Confront the world, Aundrea. You're alive. Be proud of the strong woman you are and stop hiding behind your wig."
- Amanda Maxlyn

127. "Cancer is the be-all and end-all of the sport, and the only thing you can do is show up to the game with your jersey on."
- Colleen Hoover

128. "The failure to think positively can weigh on a cancer patient like a second disease."
- Barbara Ehrenreich

129. "Sometimes even to live is an act of
courage."
- Lucius Annaeus Seneca

130. "Cancer... the process of creation
gone wild, I thought."
- Philip K. Dick

131. "What to do if you find yourself stuck in a crack in the ground underneath a giant boulder you can't move, with no hope of rescue. Consider how lucky you are that life has been good to you so far. Alternatively, if life hasn't been good to you so far, which given your current circumstances seems more likely, consider how lucky you are that it won't be troubling you much longer."
- Douglas Adams

132. "A man is happy so long as he chooses to be happy."
- Aleksandr Solzhenitsyn

133. "A life touched by cancer is not a life destroyed by cancer."
- Drew Boswel

134. "Births and cancer treatments are so expensive, it's a luxury to live, a privilege to die."
- J. Andrew Schrecker

135. "Growth for the sake of growth is the ideology of the cancer cell."
- Edward Abbey

136. "I started to walk the day I was told I was dying of cancer. I believe walking has kept me alive. I live with a constant, pressing awareness of death. Once I start to walk, I am not afraid anymore; all is well."
- Edie Littlefield Sundby

137. "Cancer does not stop your life, giving up your dreams or your goals, it is simply a parameter to manage, no more, no less than all the other parameters of life."
- Gérard Bourrat

138. "Relapse doesn't have to be part of recovery any more than return has to be part of cancer."
- Toni Sorenson

139. "What does not kill us makes us stronger."
- Friedrich Nietzsche

140. "If I keep grinning maybe my inoperable colon cancer won't hurt so much."
- Tony Millionaire

141. "My reaction on being told that I had cancer was not what I might have expected. I was relieved to finally know what I had to deal with and calm at the possibility of fading away. It seemed to me I had already lived a full life, like a well-plotted novel that reaches a satisfactory conclusion. I had known deep friendship, true love, loss, and sorrow. I had felt at one with nature and at home in the city. And, critically, I had discovered both a creative capacity within myself and inner discipline to put it to work. I had become a whole person."
- Peter Korn

142. "Without hair, A queen is still a queen."
- Prajakta Mhadnak

143. "People wonder why cancer exists when it is just a clever method to teach people lessons about love and loss. It borrows time or steals it depending on the needs of Heaven. It is a vehicle to get us where we need to be. It calls us home because something needs us there."
- Kate McGahan

144. "I decided right then and there that no matter what cancer did to me I would continue to move. Movement was what the physical body was designed to do; it was how it coped and functioned. Movement was vitality. It was life. I would move. Always. No matter what. Until my last breath, I would move."
- Edie Littlefield Sundby

145. "Whether you're a mother or father, or a husband or a son, or a niece or a nephew or uncle, breast cancer doesn't discriminate.'
- Stephanie McMahon

146. "Did you notice the smile on a cancer patient's face after the last treatment? That's the smile you want on your face."
- Lawrence Wray

147. "I began to realize that coming in such close contact with my own mortality had changed both nothing and everything. Before my cancer was diagnosed, I knew that someday I would die, but I didn't know when. After the diagnosis, I knew that someday I would die, but I didn't know when. But now I knew it acutely. The problem wasn't really a scientific one. The fact of death is unsettling. Yet there is no other way to live."
- Paul Kalanithi

148. "Cancer is a journey, but you walk the road alone. There are many places to stop along the way and get nourishment—you just have to be willing to take it."
- Emily Hollenberg

149. "We normally know we're getting older when the only thing we want for our birthday is not to be reminded; unless you're a cancer survivor! Then we love people reminding us!"
- Chris Geiger

150. "I'm going to beat this cancer or die trying."
- Michael Landon

Closing Remark

As we conclude this compilation of inspiring quotes from remarkable cancer survivors, we extend our heartfelt wishes for healing, strength, and unwavering resilience to all those touched by the challenges of cancer. May these words continue to serve as a source of hope, courage, and empowerment in your journey towards brighter days ahead.

www.ingramcontent.com/pod-product-compliance
Lightning Source LLC
Chambersburg PA
CBHW061003260726

48661CB00005B/2038